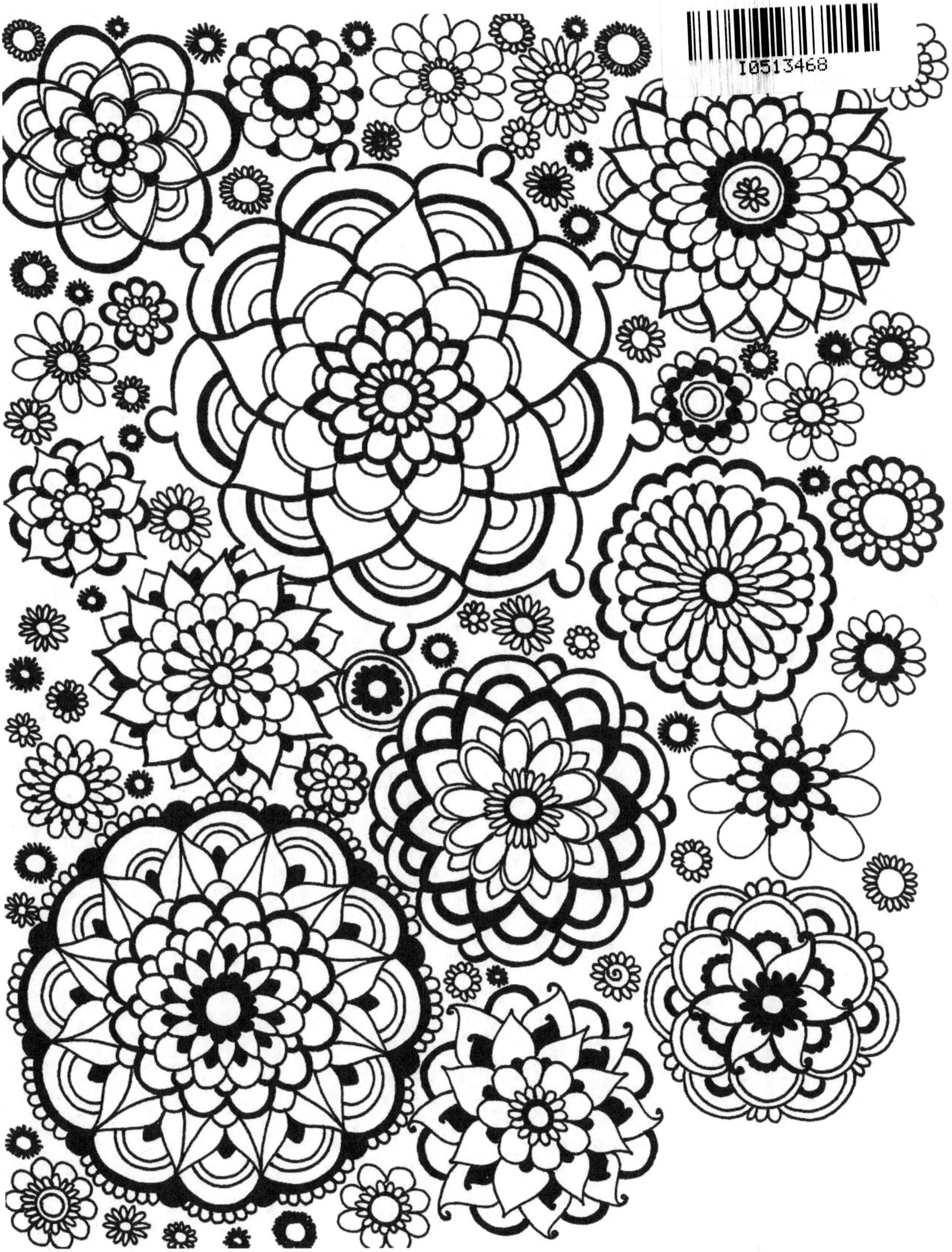

I0513468

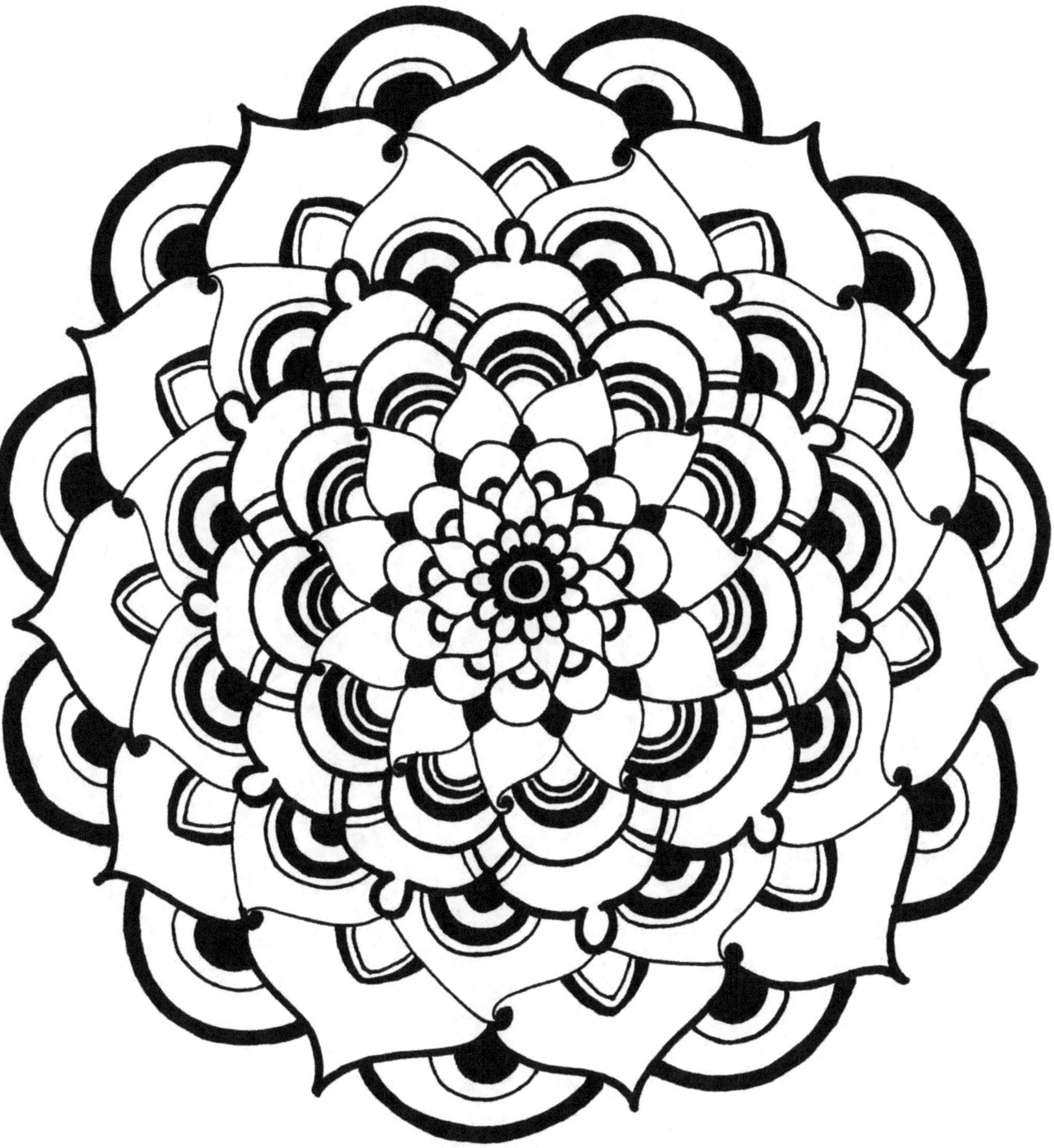

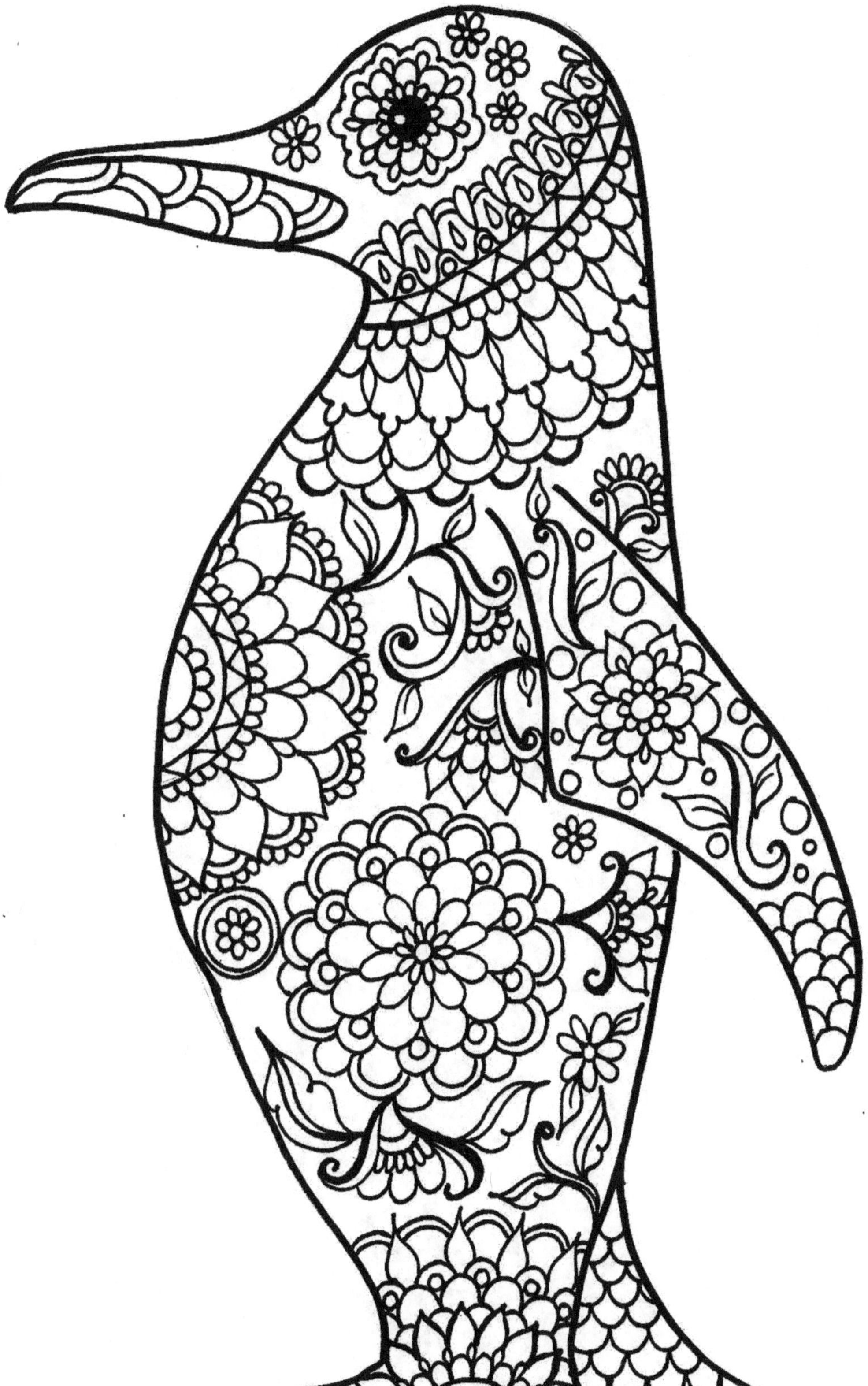

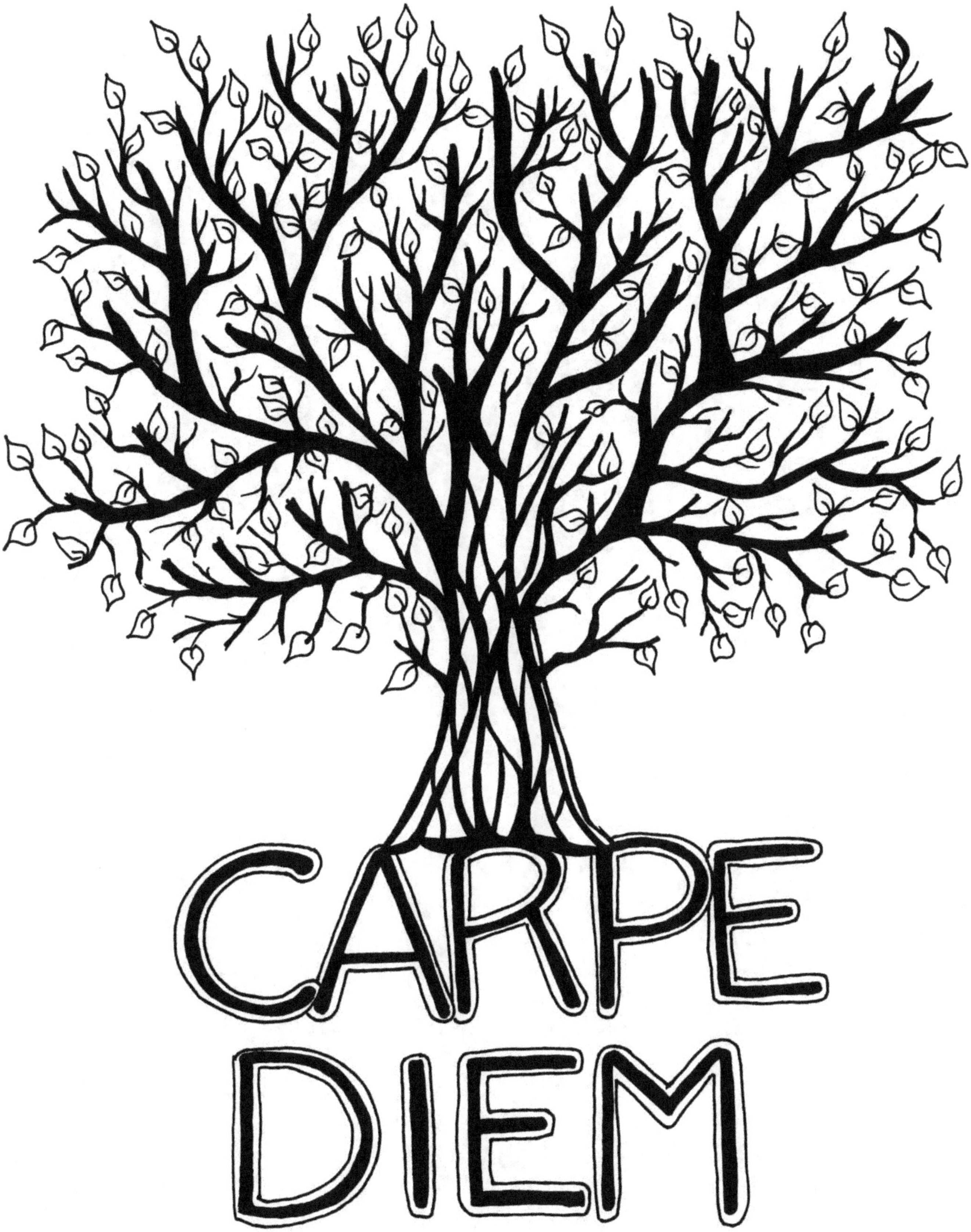
CARPE
DIEM

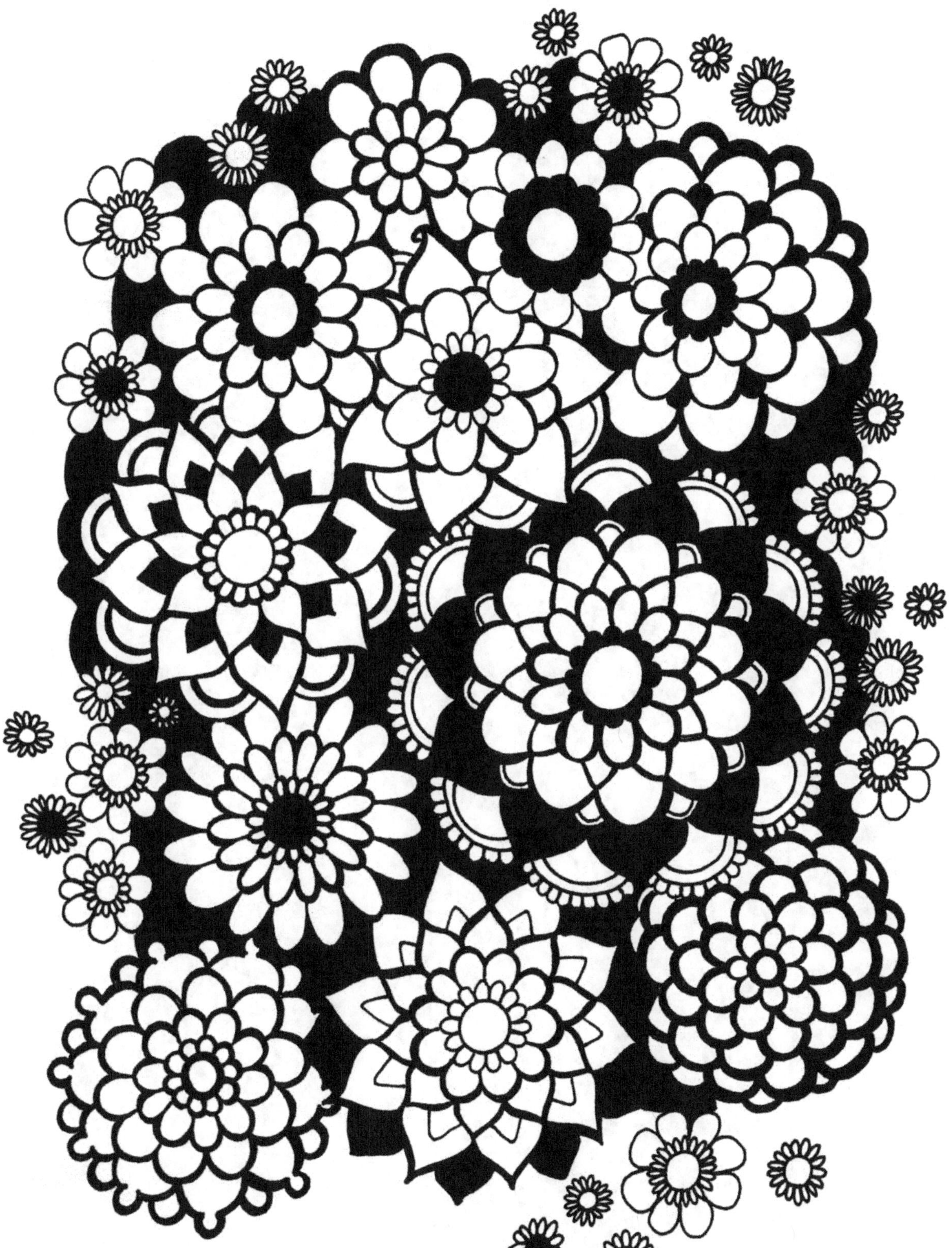

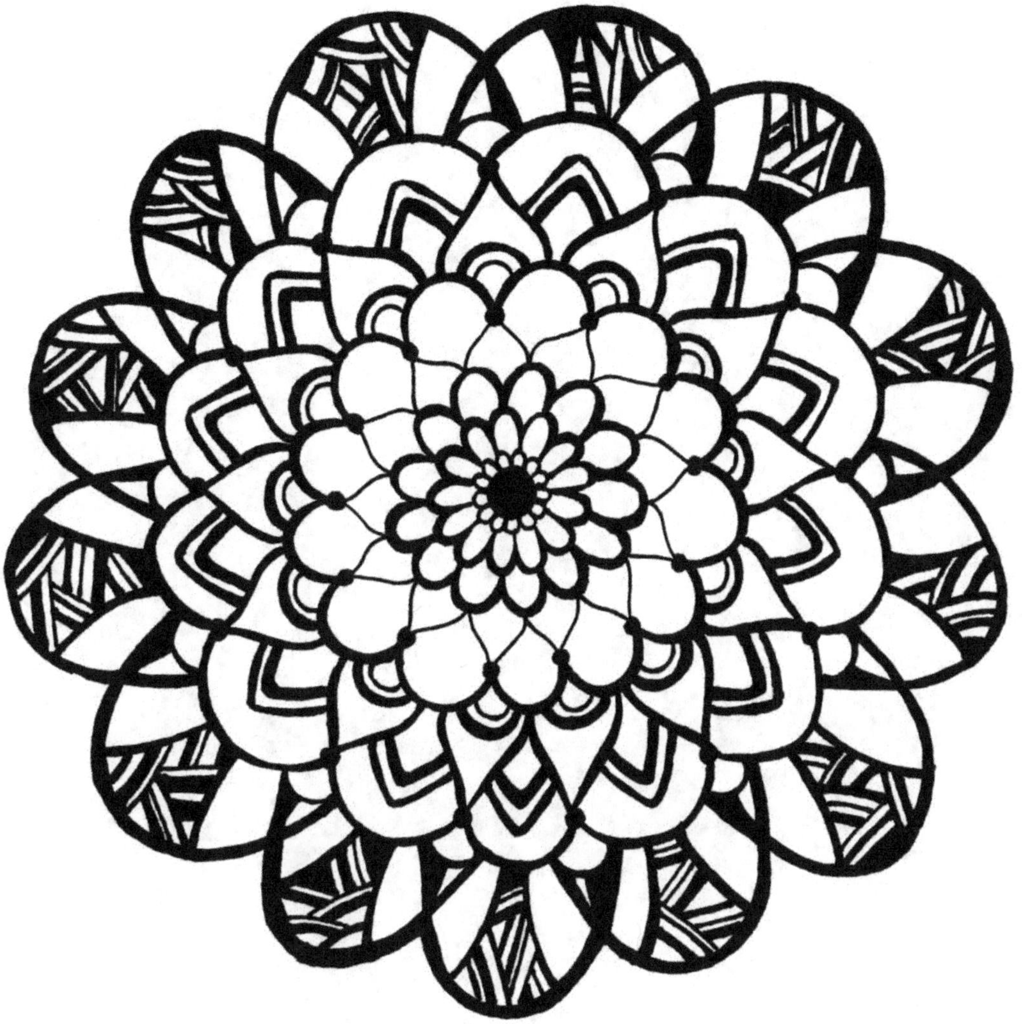

Namaste

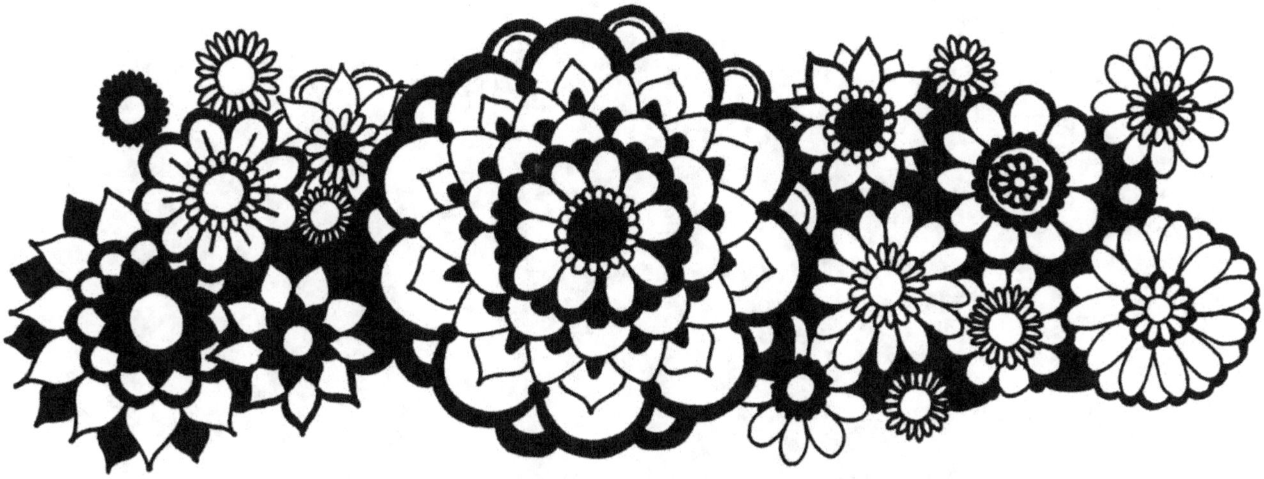

CARPE DIEM

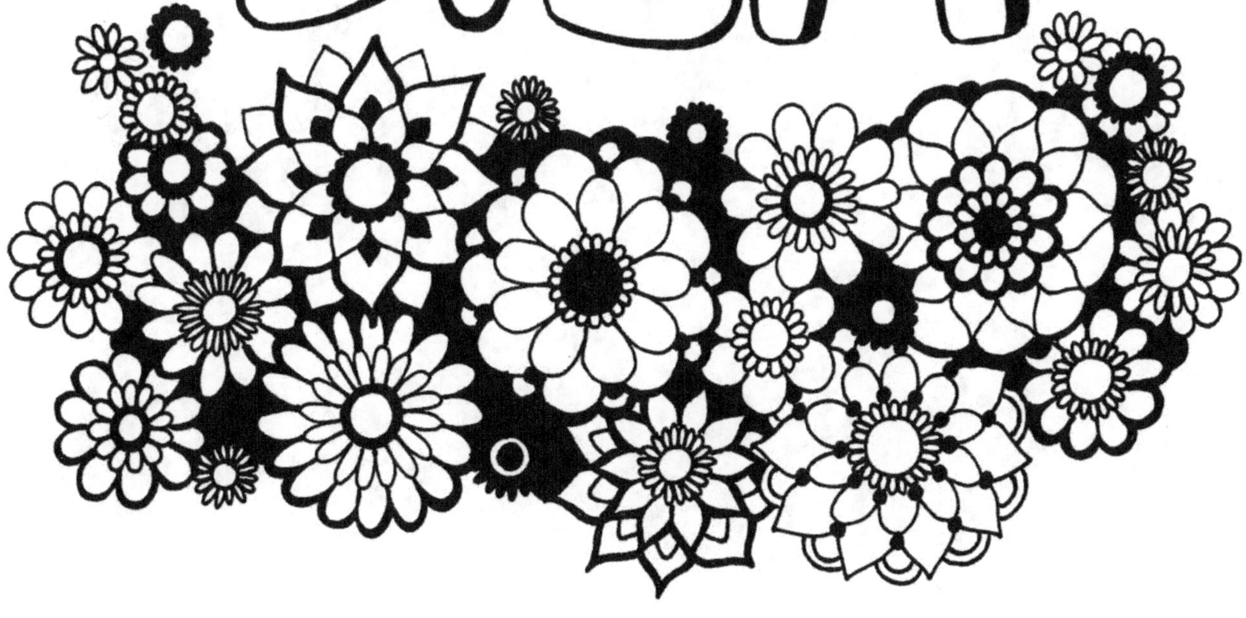

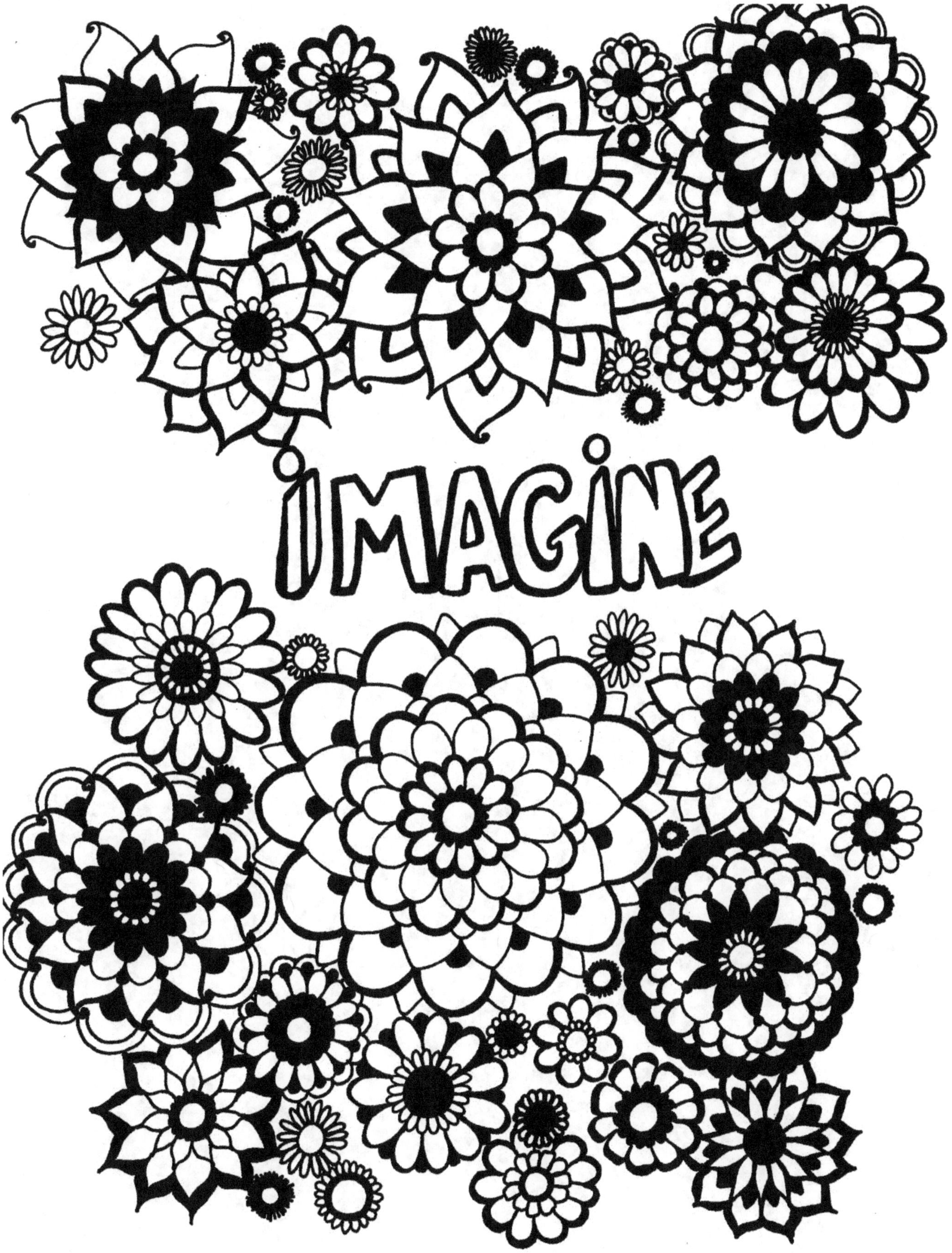
IMAGINE

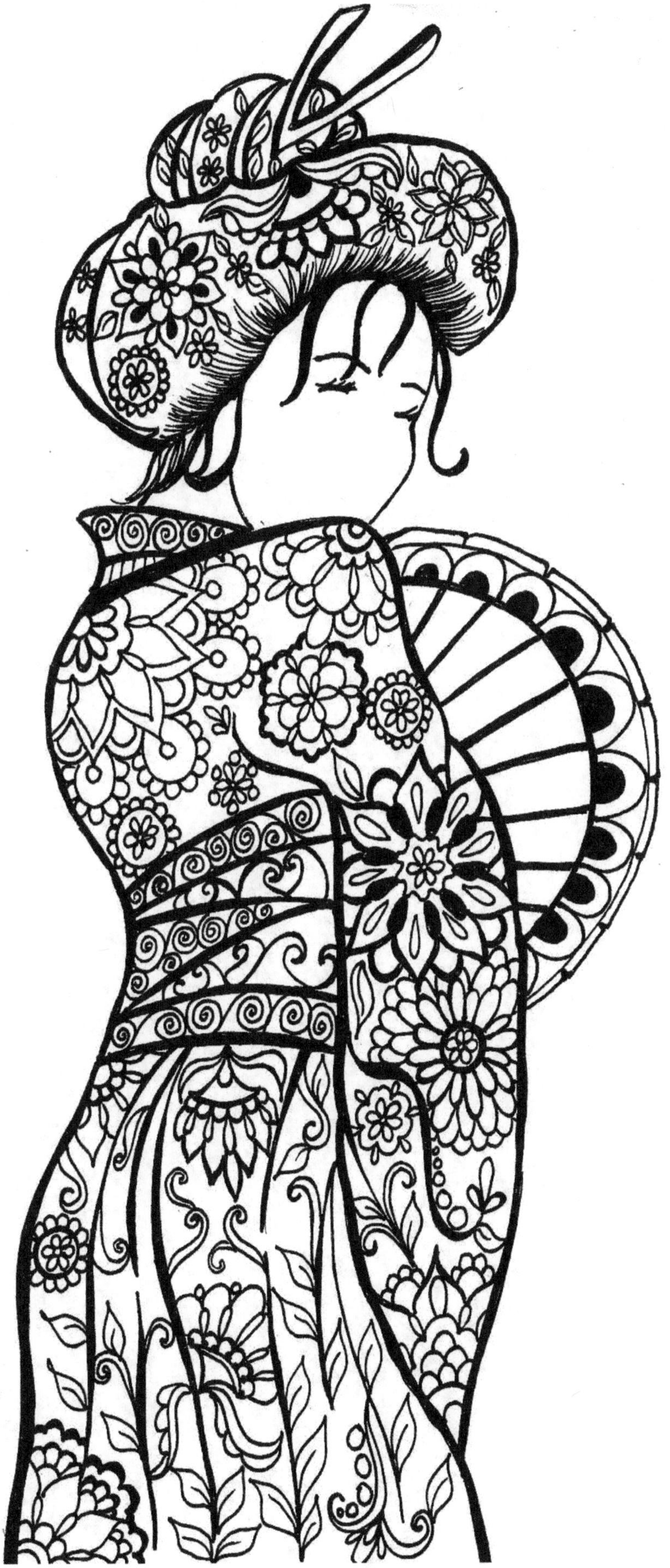

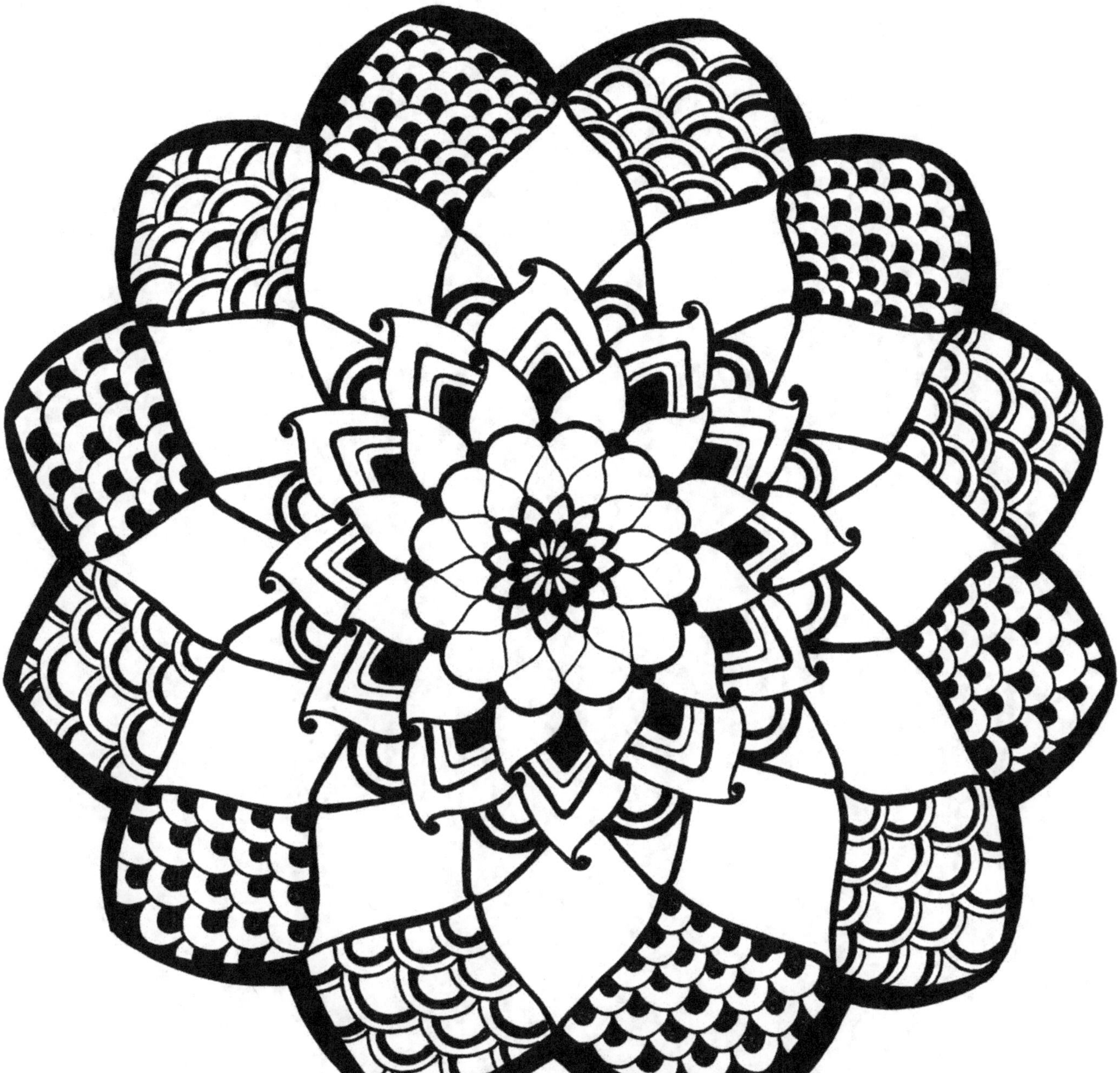

NAMASTE

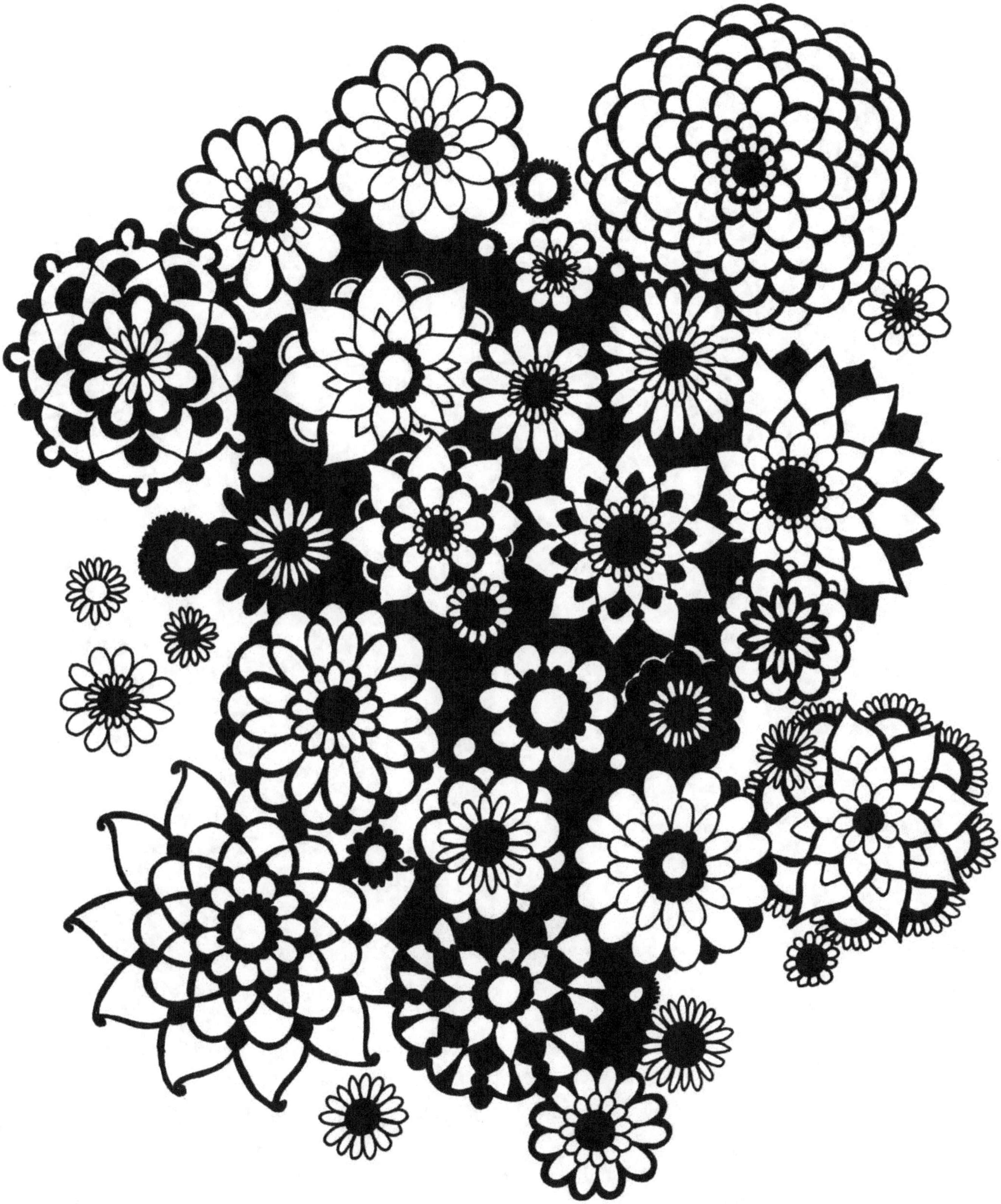

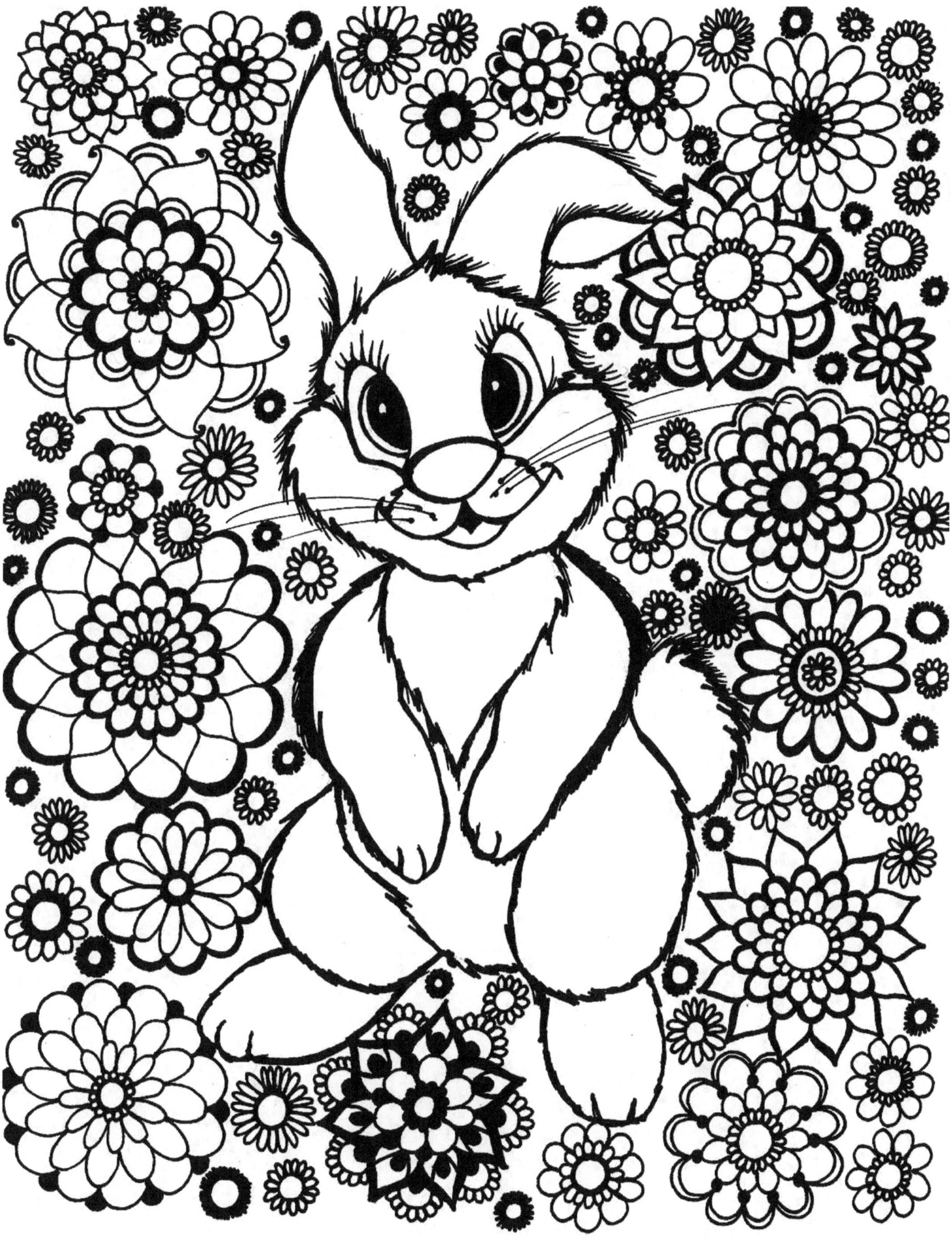

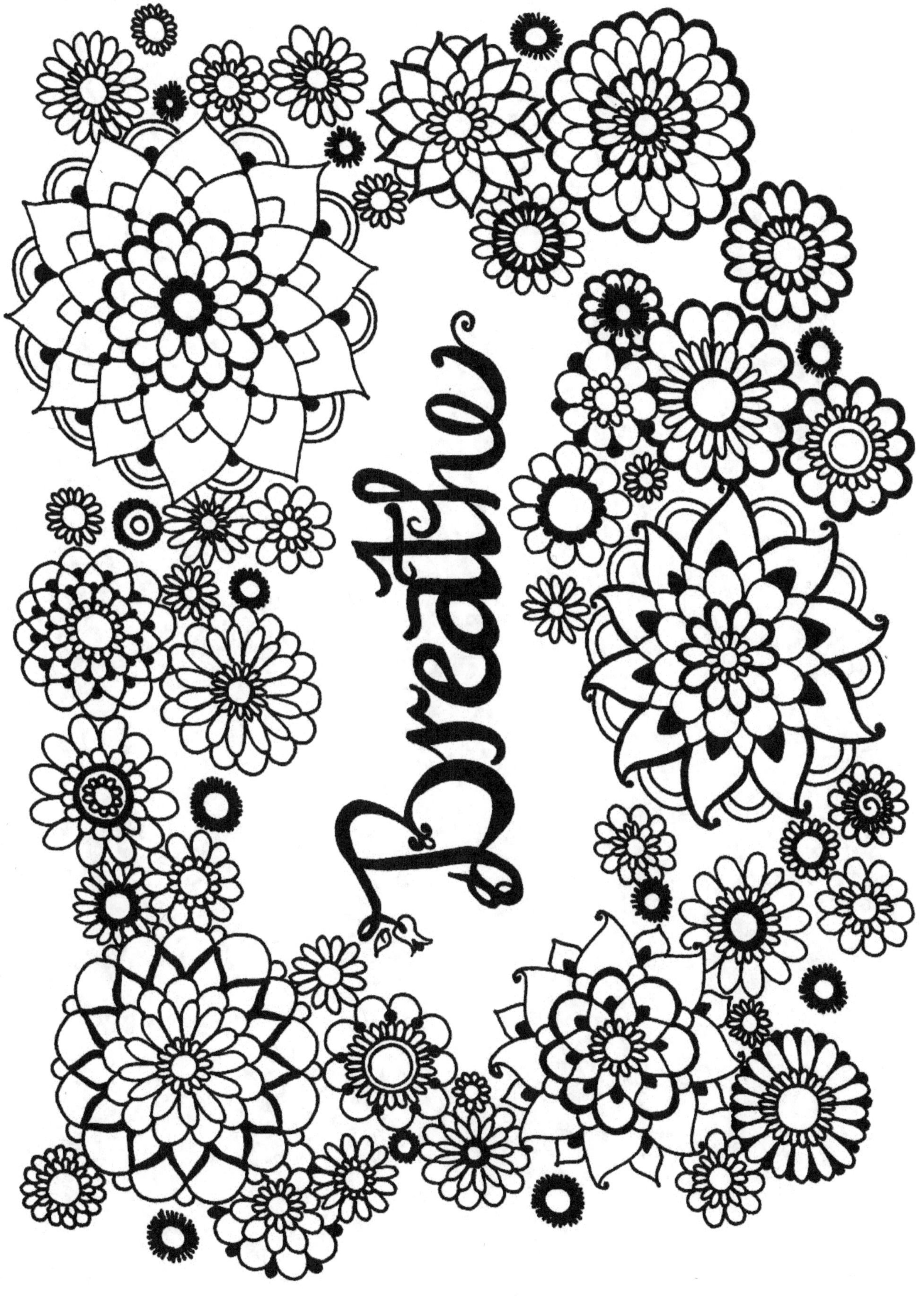
Breathe

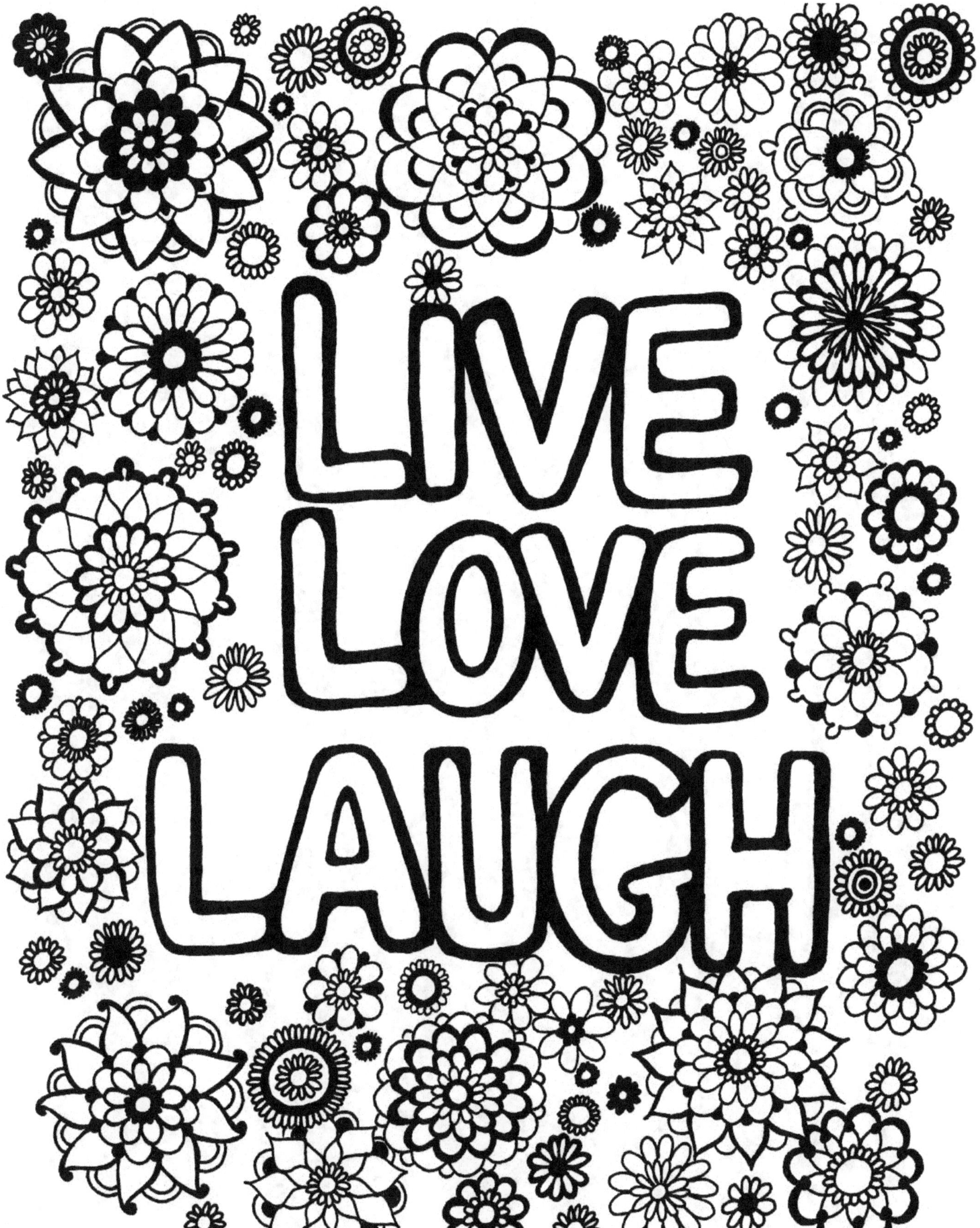
LIVE
LOVE
LAUGH

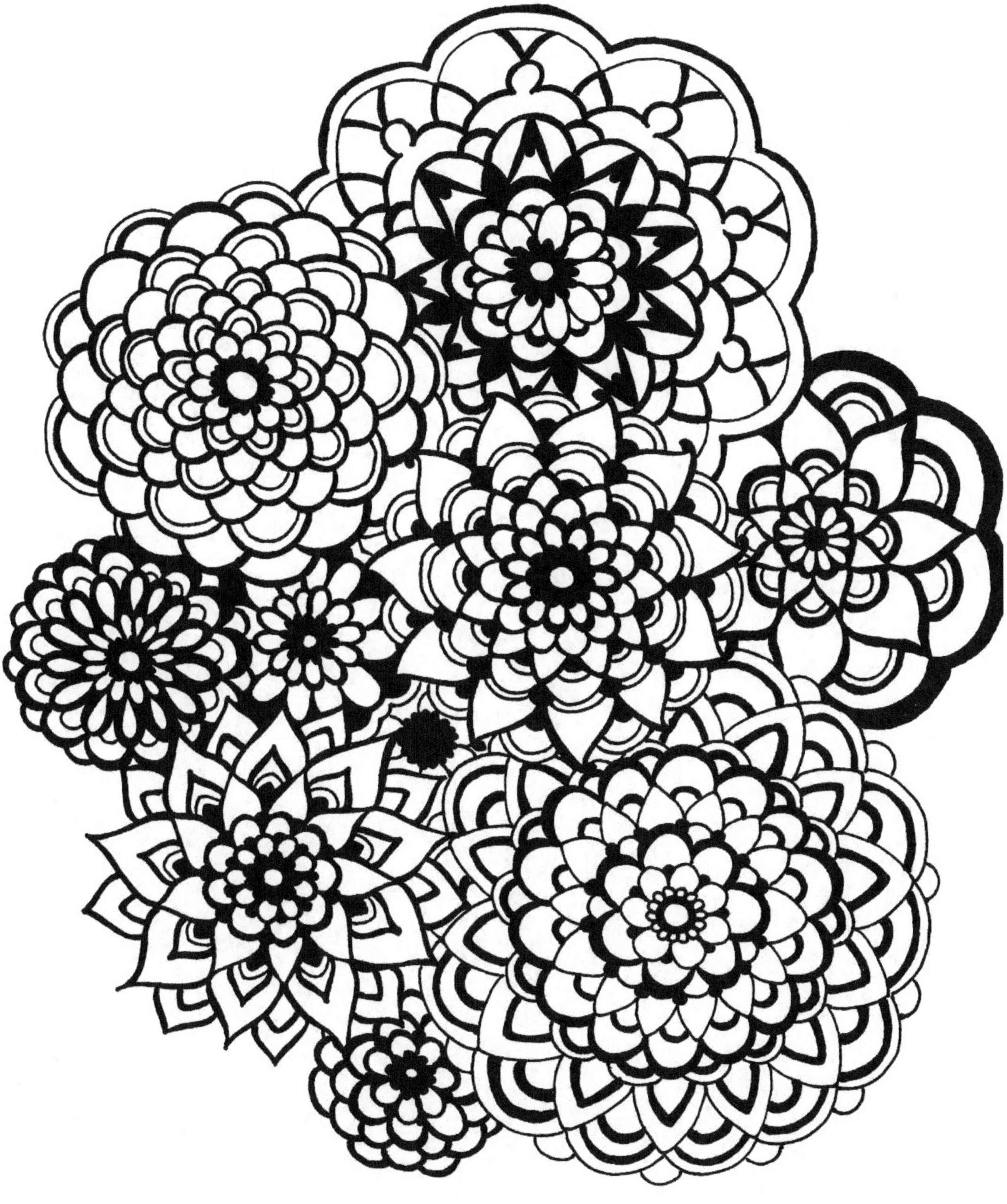

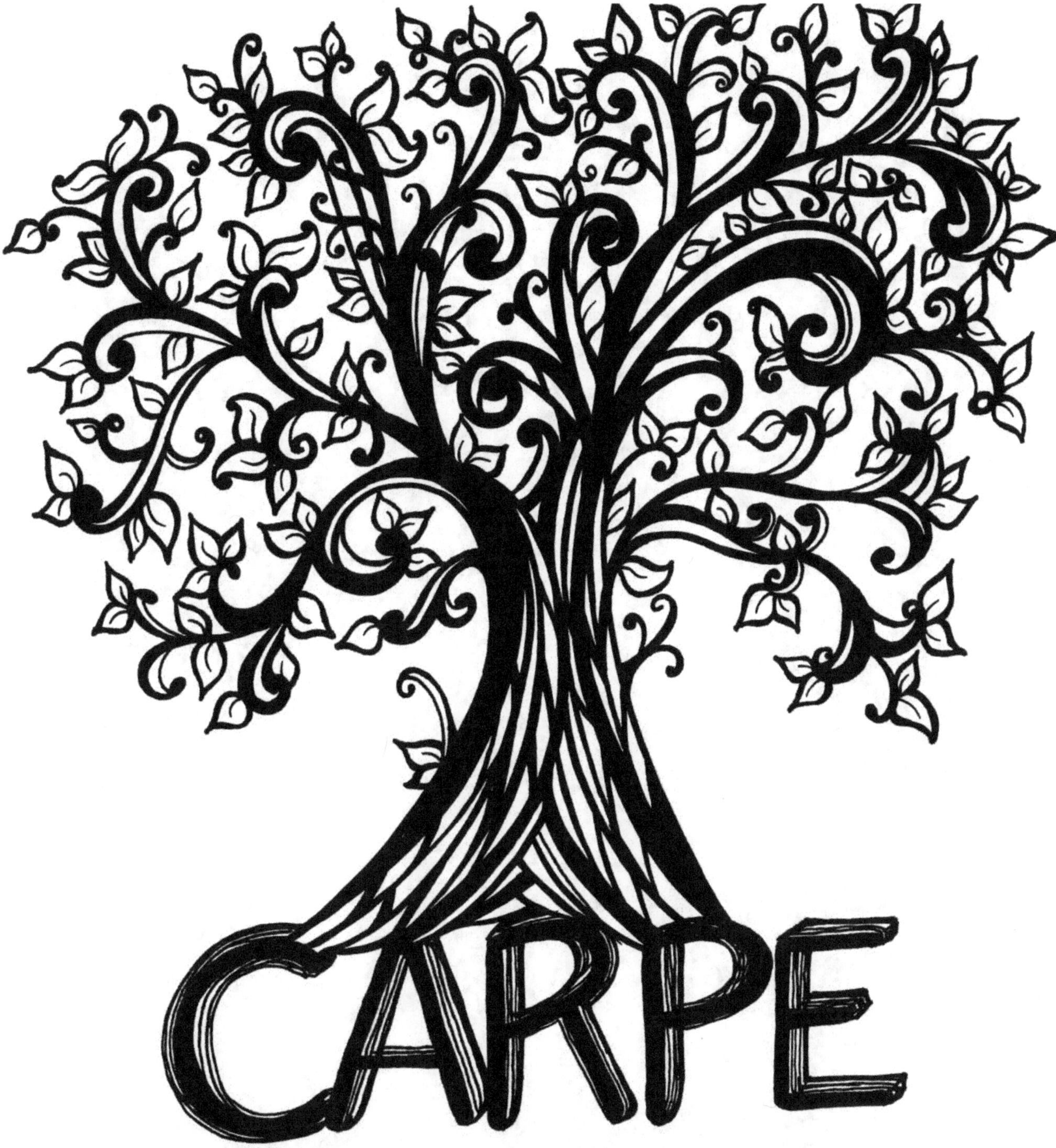
CARPE
DIEM

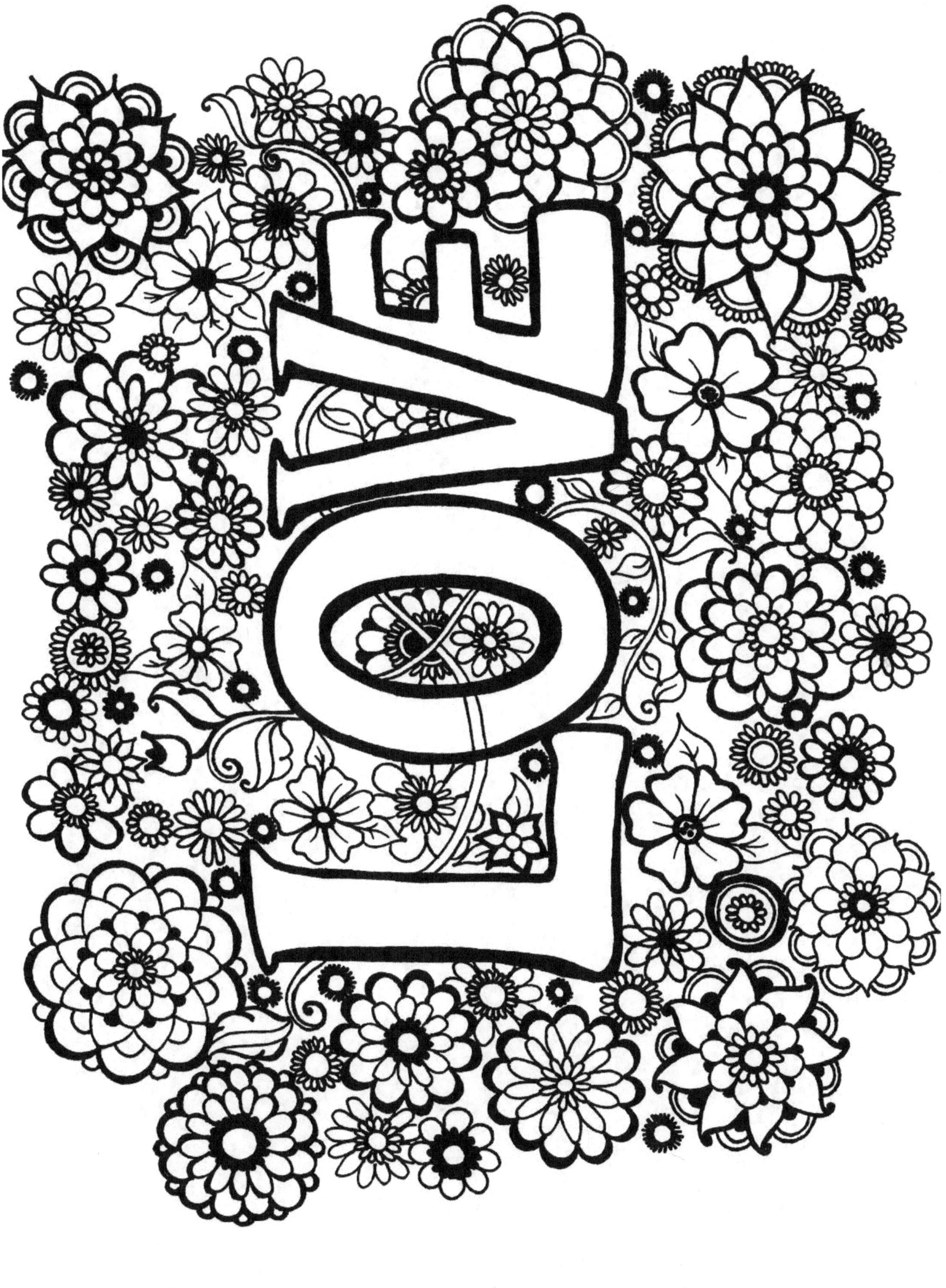
LOVE

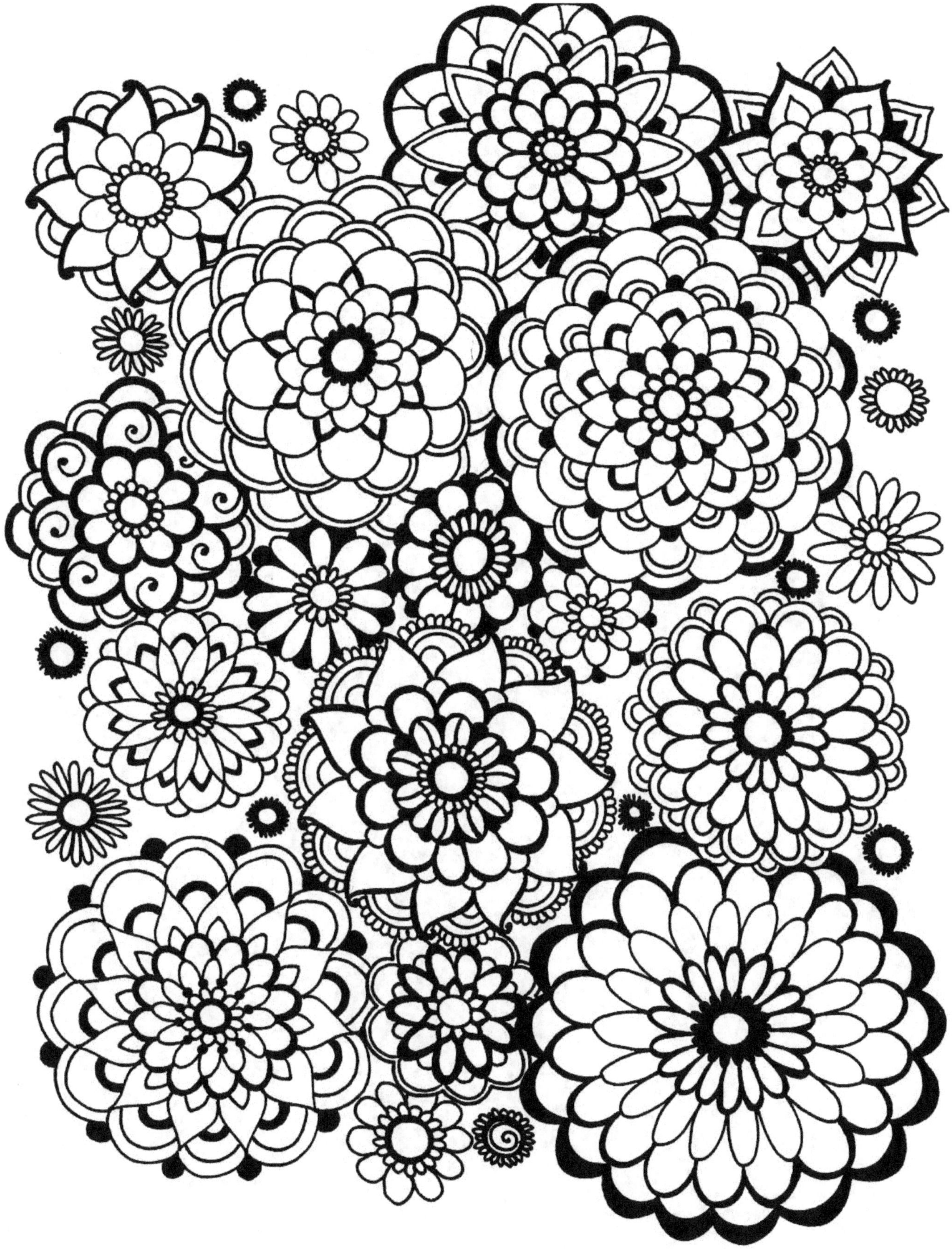

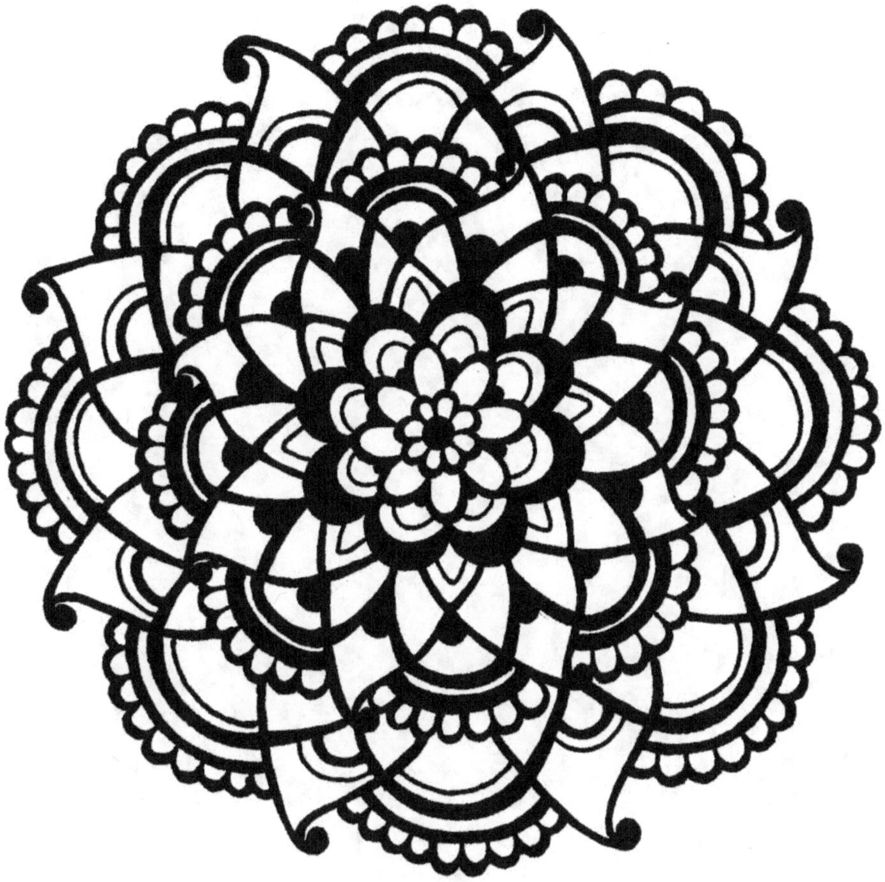

CARPE DIEM

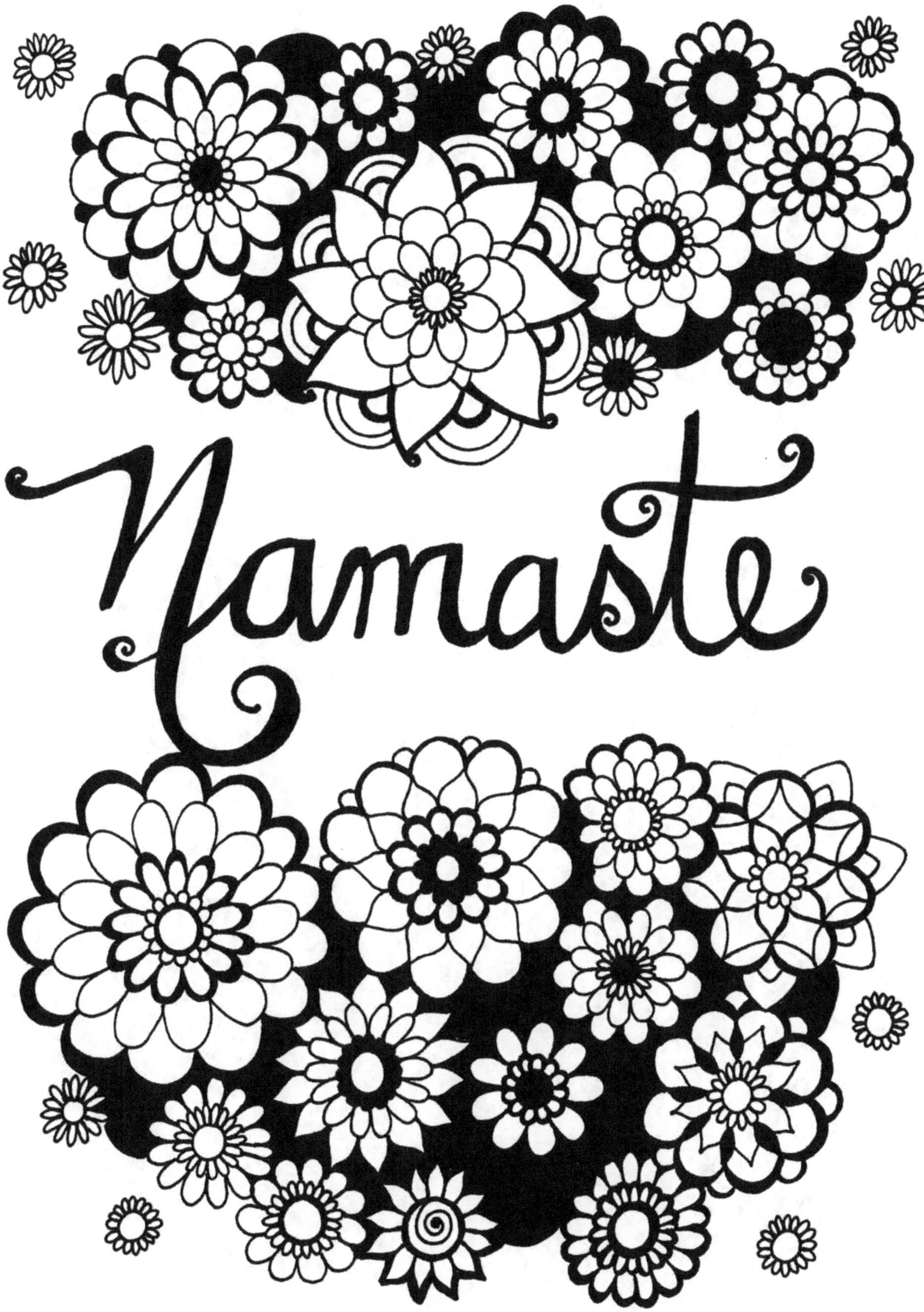
Namaste

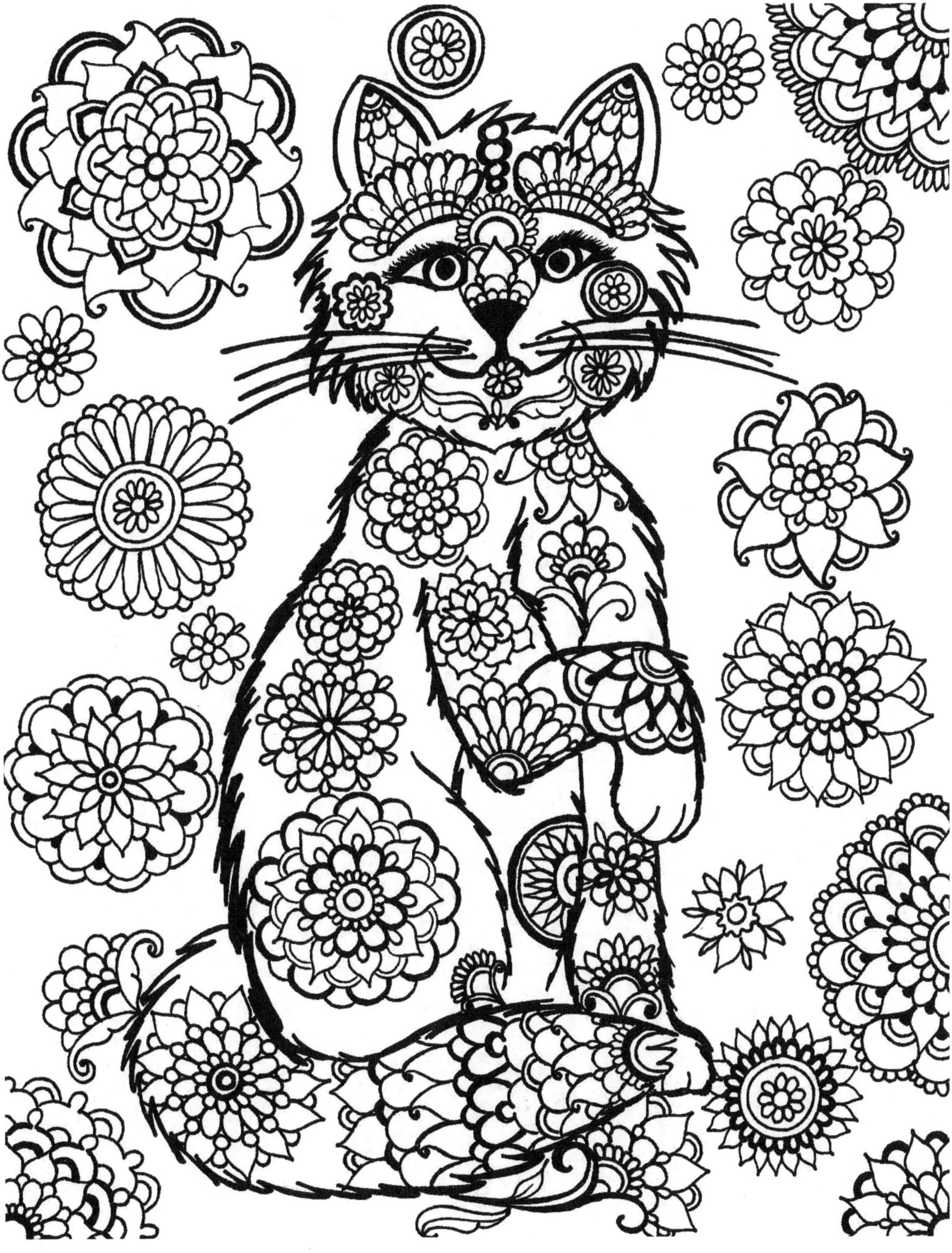

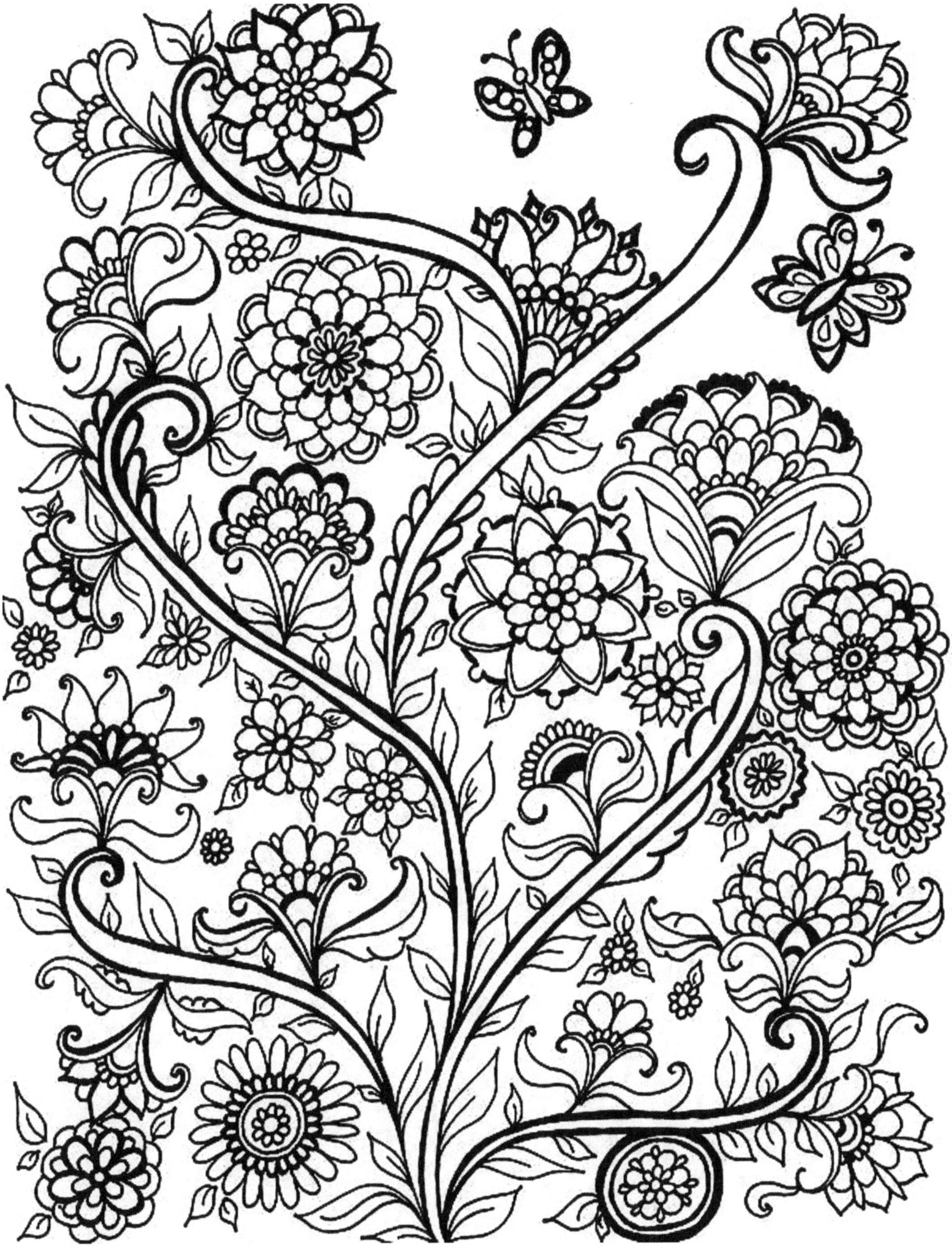

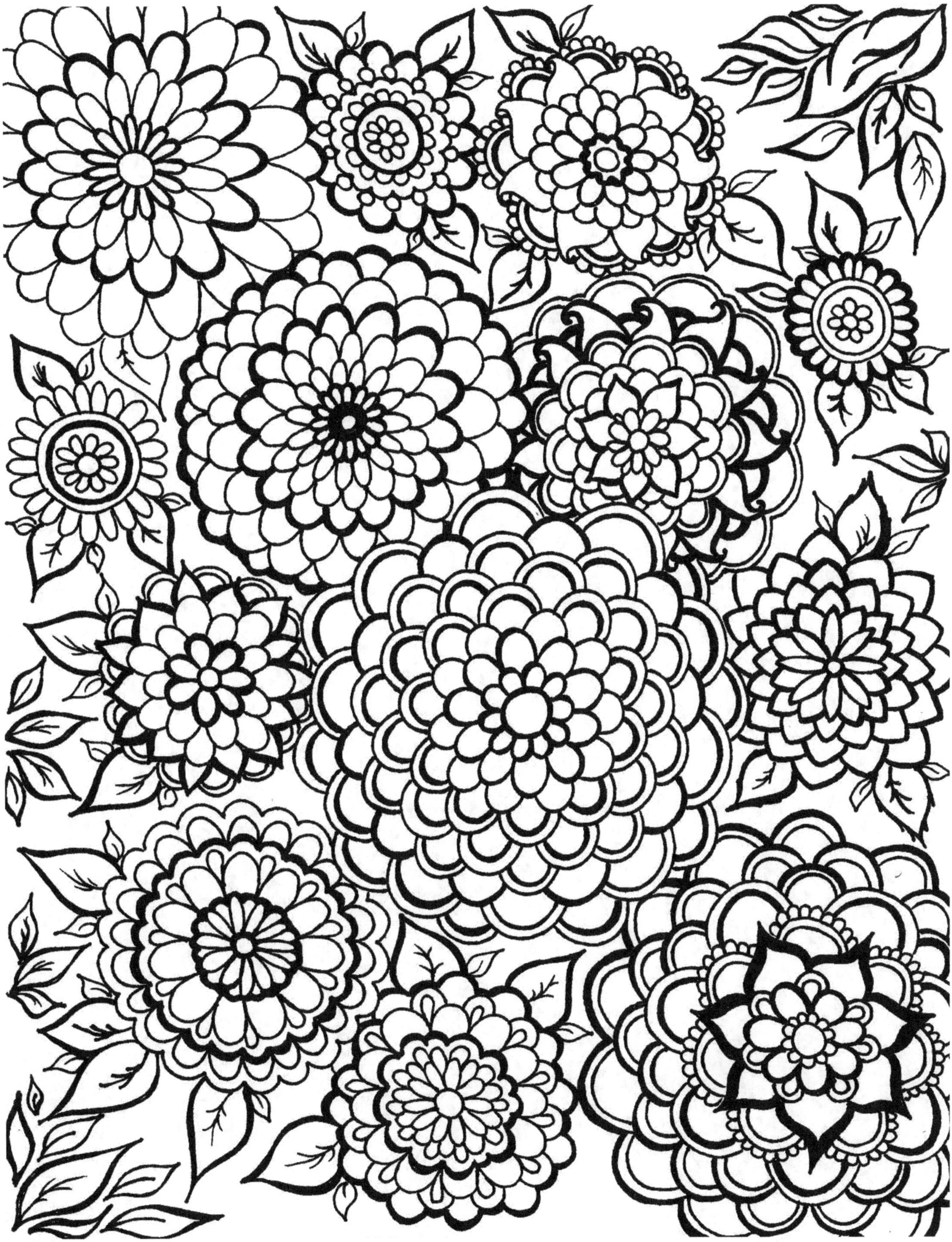

www.ingramcontent.com/pod-product-compliance
Lightning Source LLC
Chambersburg PA
CBHW062234220526
45471CB00009B/3481
9781986874205